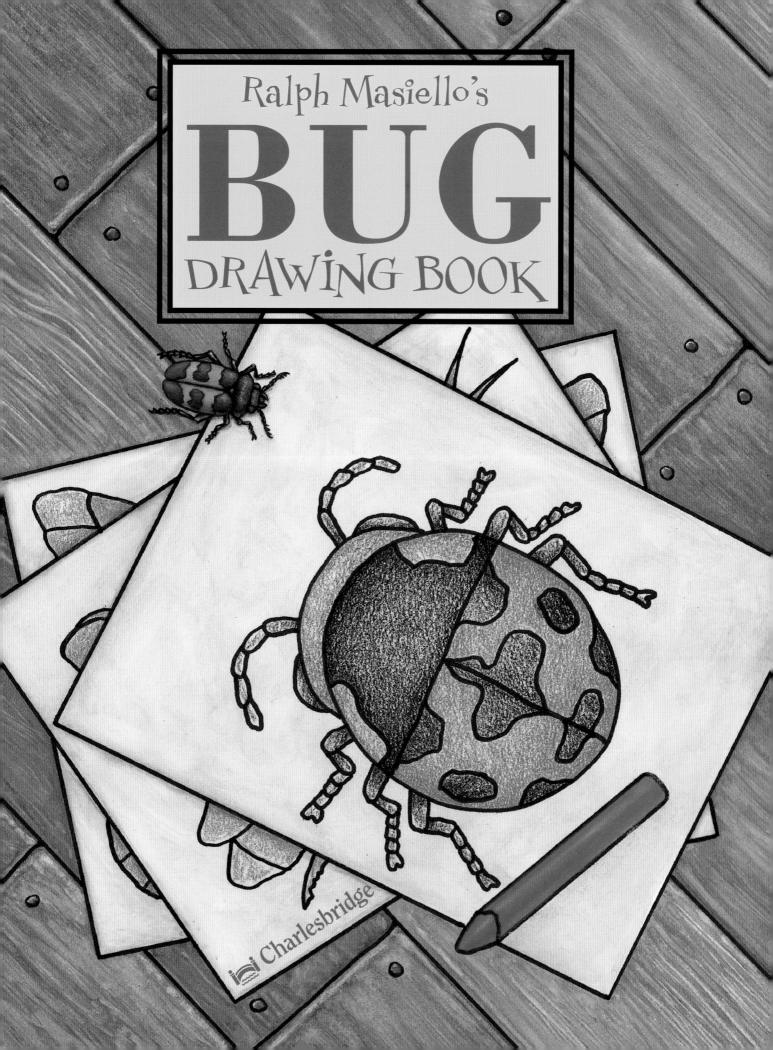

For my nephews, Billy and Jonathan,
and my niece, Jenna—R. M.

Other books illustrated by Ralph Masiello:
The Dinosaur Alphabet Book
The Extinct Alphabet Book
The Flag We Love
The Frog Alphabet Book
The Icky Bug Alphabet Book
The Icky Bug Counting Book
The Skull Alphabet Book
The Yucky Reptile Alphabet Book
Cuenta los insectos

Published by Charlesbridge
85 Main Street
Watertown, MA 02472
(617) 926-0329
www.charlesbridge.com

Library of Congress Cataloging-in-Publication Data
Masiello, Ralph.
    [Bug drawing book]
    Ralph Masiello's bug drawing book / written and illustrated by Ralph Masiello.
        p. cm.
    ISBN 1-57091-525-3 (reinforced for library use)
    ISBN 1-57091-526-1 (softcover)
1. Insects in art—Juvenile literature. 2. Drawing—Technique—Juvenile literature.
[1. Insects in art. 2. Drawing—Technique.] I. Title.
NC783.M38 2004
743.6'57—dc22   2003023409

Printed in China
(hc) 10 9 8 7 6 5 4 3 2 1
(sc) 10 9 8 7 6 5 4 3 2 1

Illustrations done in mixed media
Display type set in Couchlover, designed by Chank, Minneapolis, Minnesota;
    text type set in Goudy
Color separated, printed, and bound by Jade Productions
Production supervision by Brian G. Walker
Designed by Susan Mallory Sherman

Hello, Fellow Artists!

Yes, that's you! Anyone can learn to draw, and this book will show you how. I've been a children's book illustrator for almost 20 years. Every year I visit schools across the country to talk to kids like you. Kids are always asking me to draw stuff. Drawing is all about knowing how to see something and then breaking it down into simple shapes and lines. Anything that seems complicated can be broken down— you just have to learn how to see. It takes practice, but with patience and by really looking carefully, you'll be able to draw anything.

By following the steps I've marked in red, you'll be able to draw all the creatures in this book. I've also included extra challenge boxes, so you can have even more fun with your drawings. My biggest hope is that when you're done you'll close the book, look at the world around you, and pick up your favorite pencil, marker, crayon, or brush. You are an artist!

Ralph

Choose your tools

pastel pencil crayon watercolor fine-tip marker colored pencil marker poster paint

Beetle

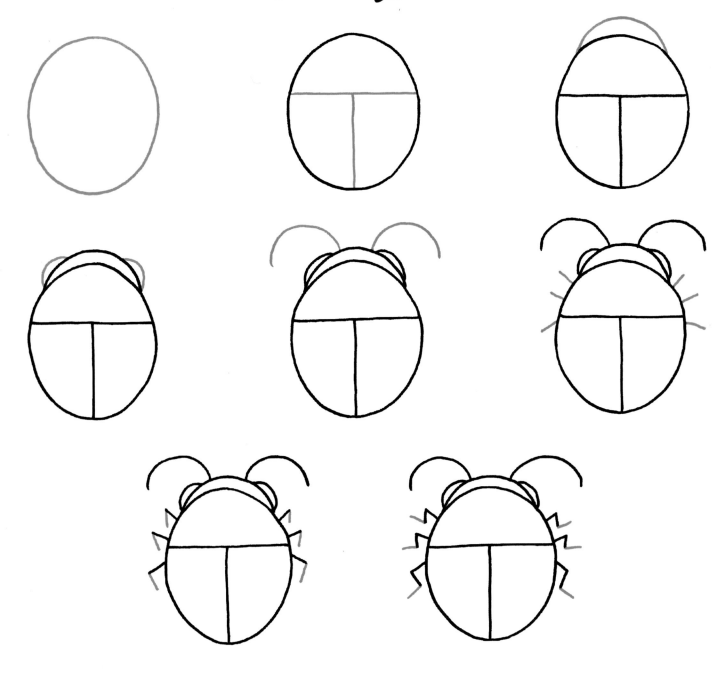

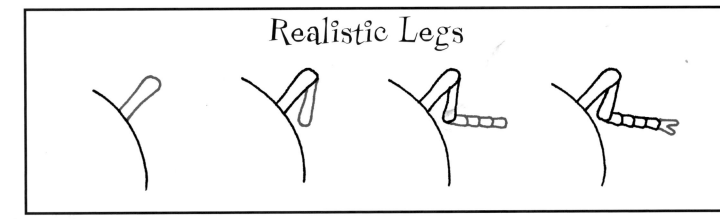

Realistic Legs

Now have fun! Color that beetle
with your favorite color.

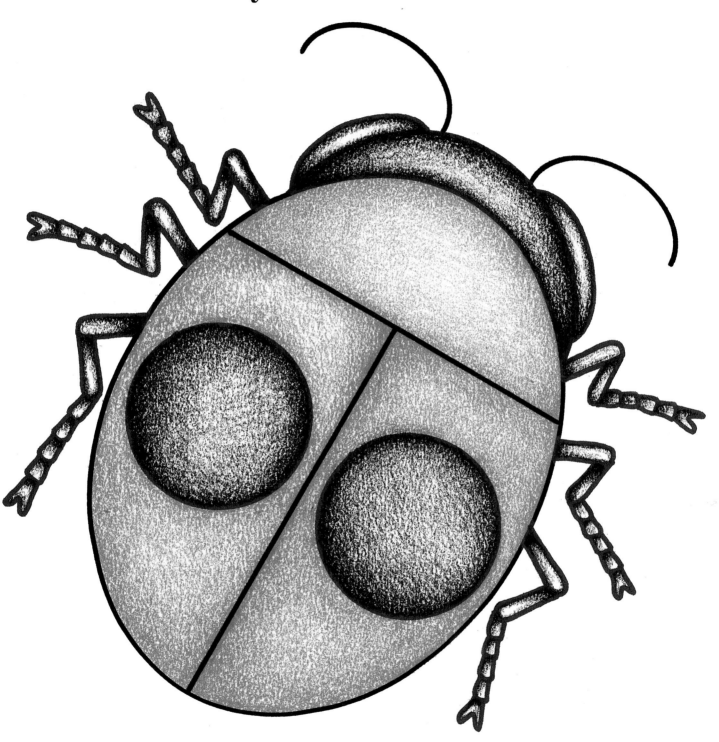

crayon

Stink Bug

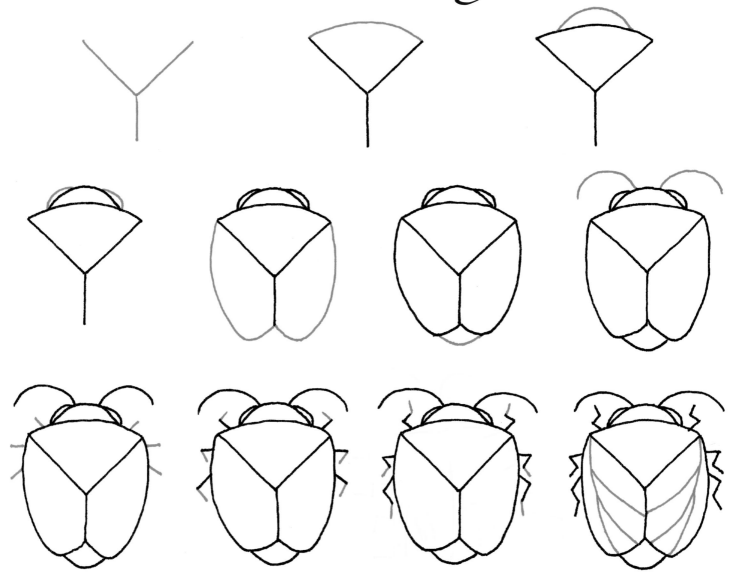

Realistic Antennae

Add some realistic legs and antennae to Mr. Stinky.

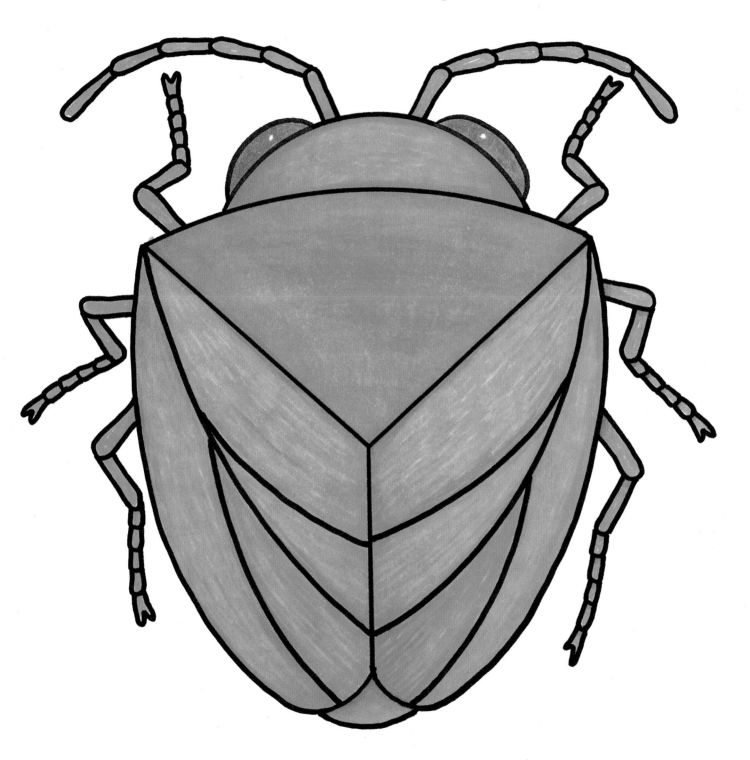

marker

Caterpillar

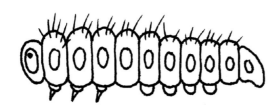
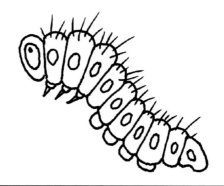

Make your caterpillar colorful.

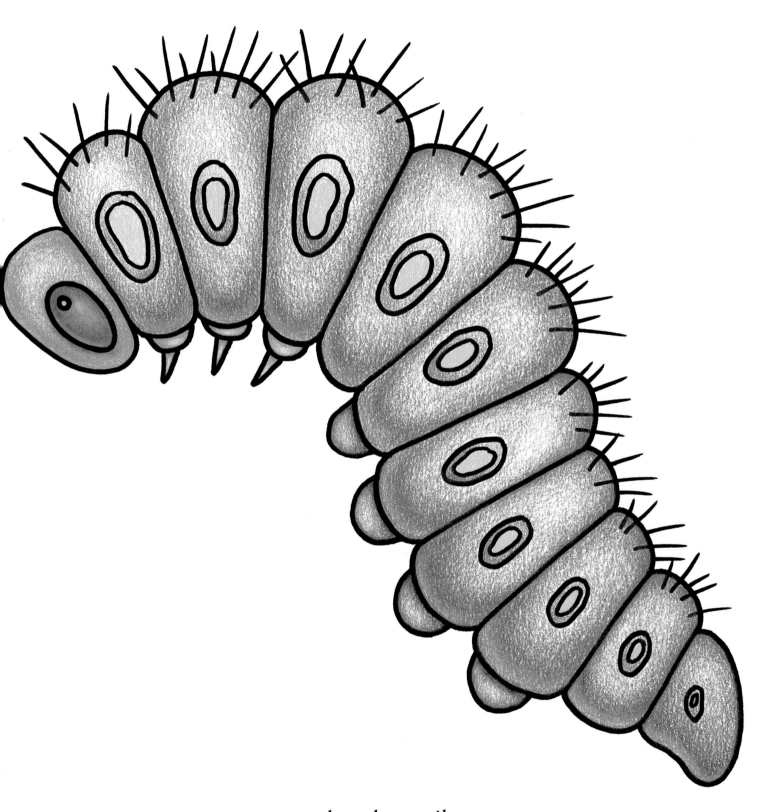

colored pencil

Chrysalis

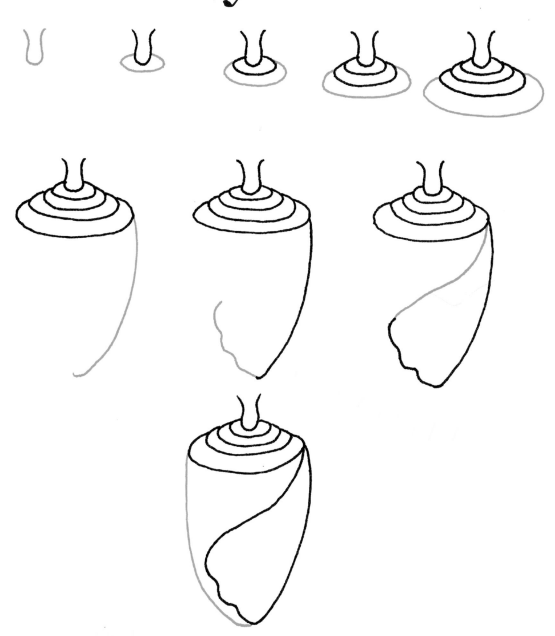

Branch and Leaves

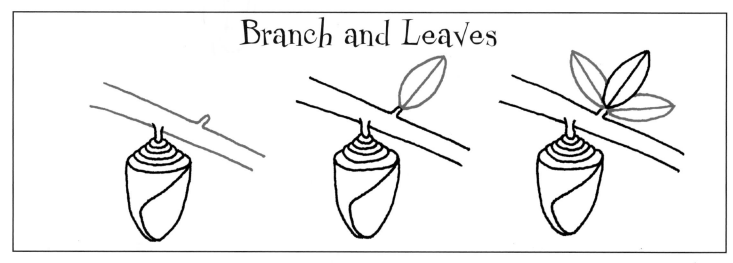

Now give that chrysalis a place to hang.

pastel pencil

Butterfly (side view)

More Wing Shapes

Make a whole life cycle: caterpillar
to chrysalis to butterfly.

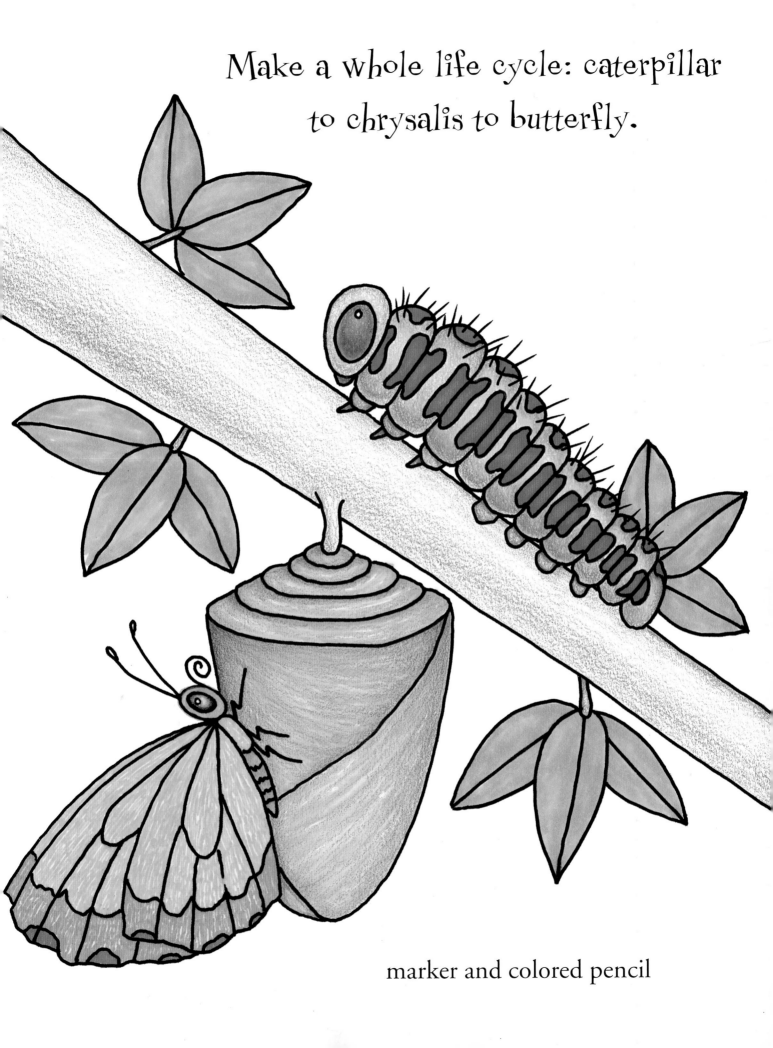

marker and colored pencil

Butterfly (top view)

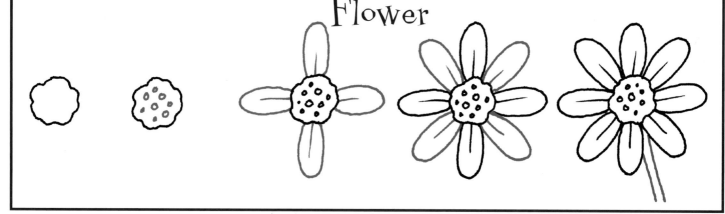

Flower

Land your butterfly gently on a flower.

poster paint

Spider

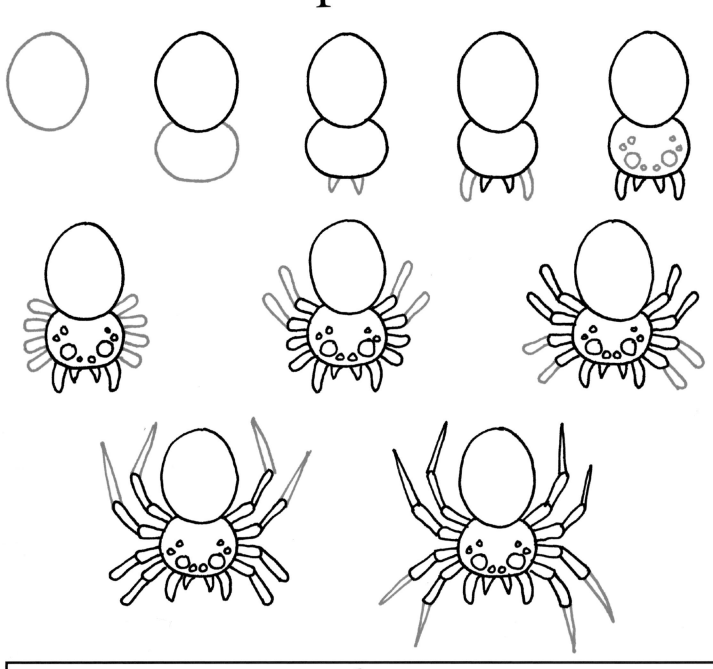

More Spiders

Hang your spider!

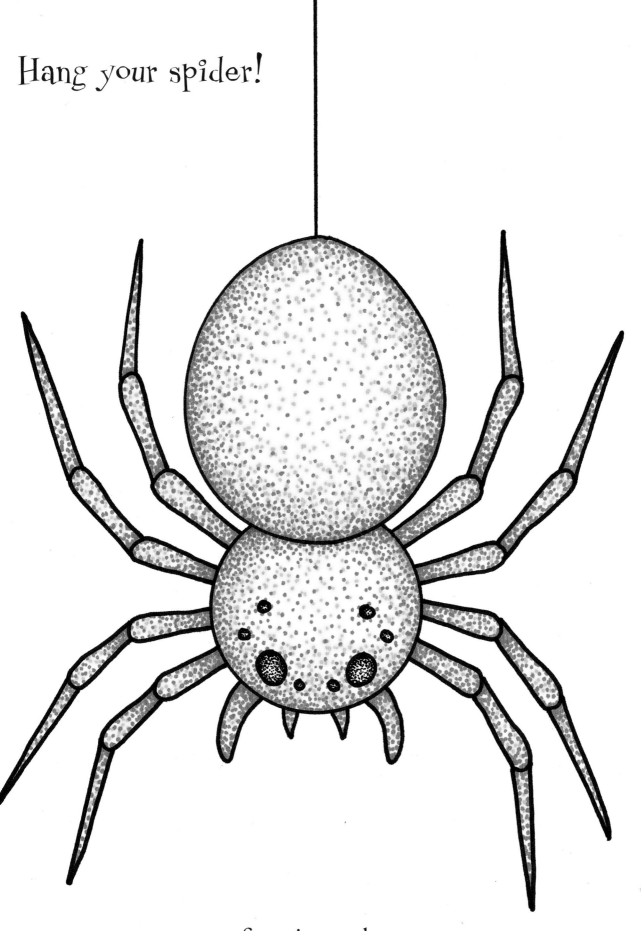

fine-tip marker

fine-tip marker and watercolor

Spider Web

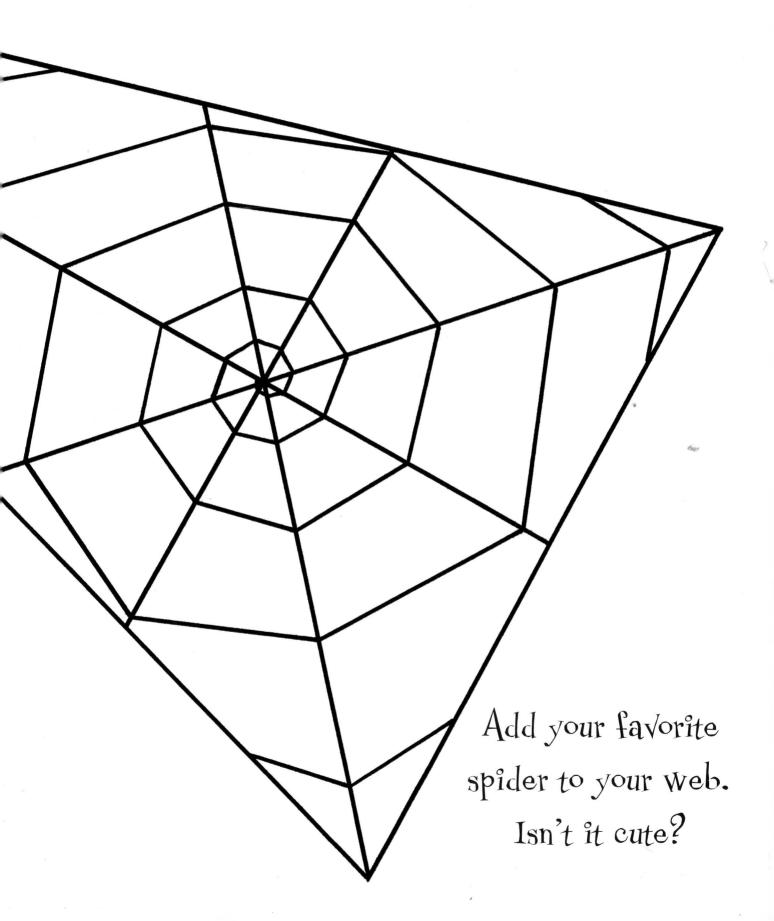

Add your favorite
spider to your web.
Isn't it cute?

Ant

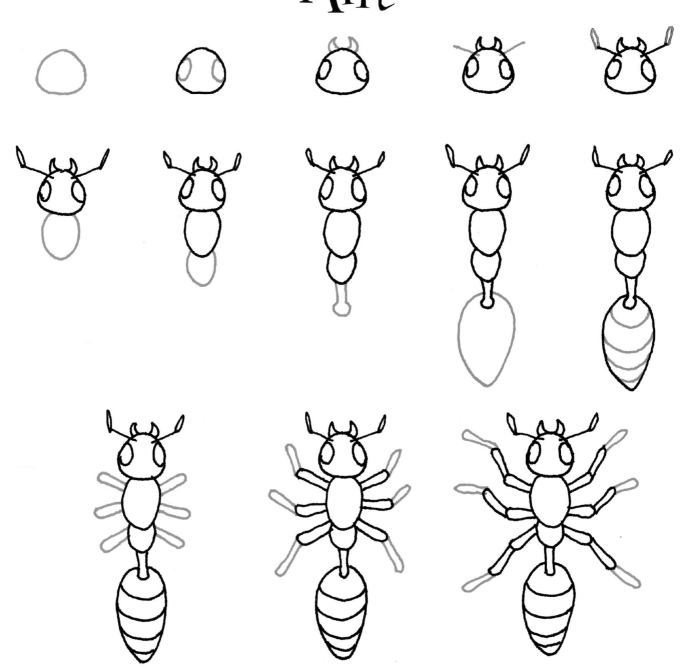

Mushroom

Let your ants creep all over that mushroom.

watercolor and
crayon

Housefly

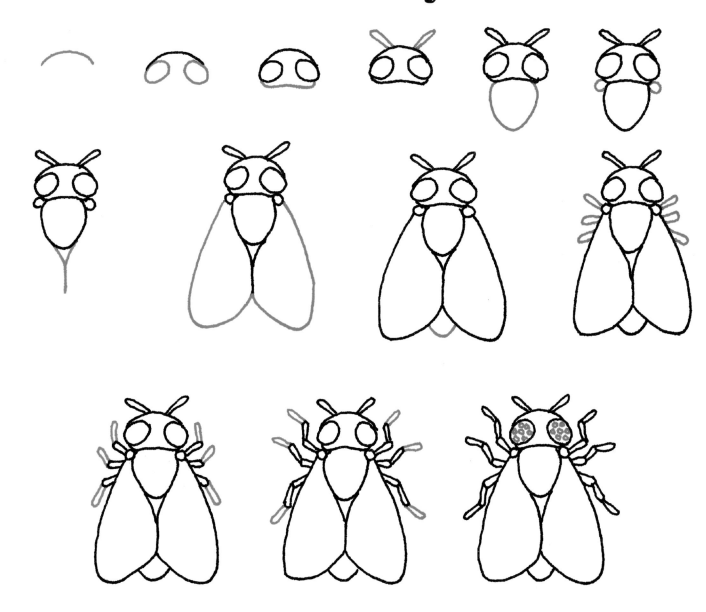

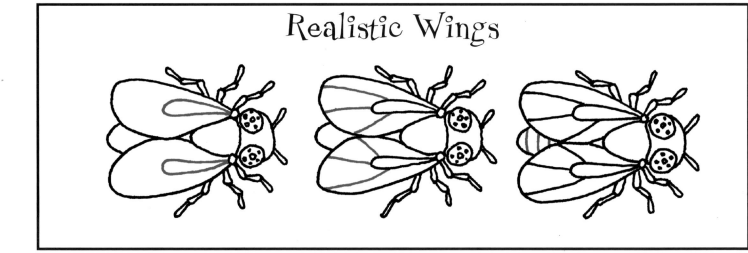

Realistic Wings

Make your fly HUGE!

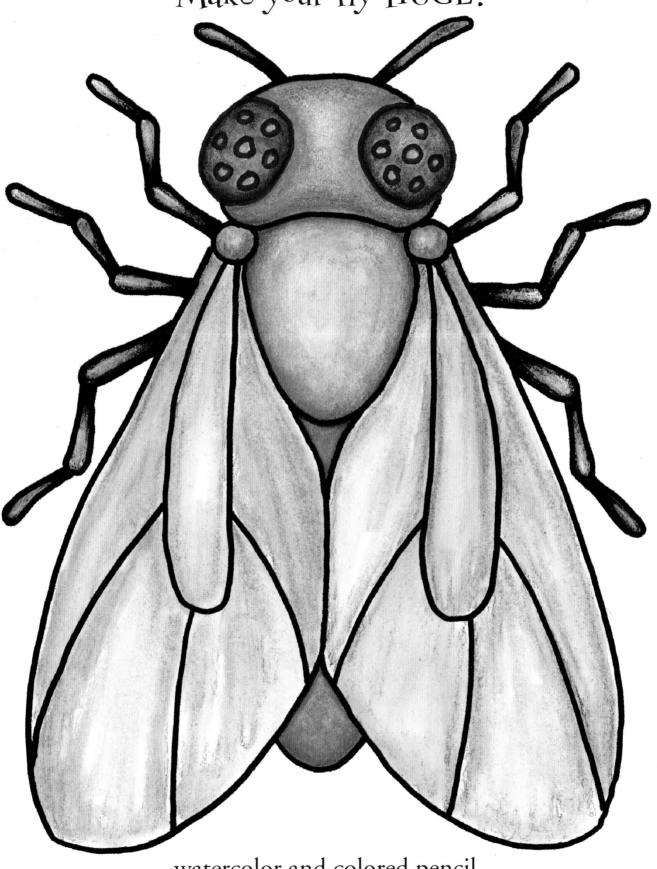

watercolor and colored pencil

Bee

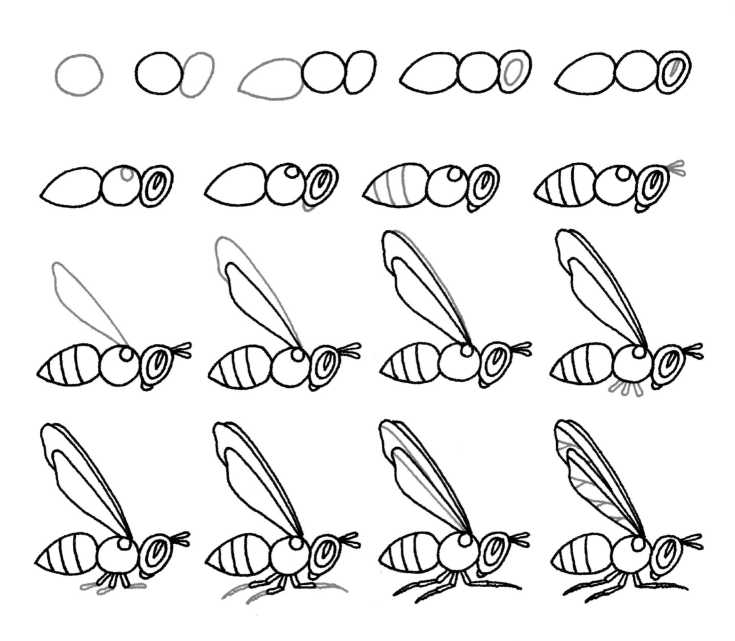

Flower

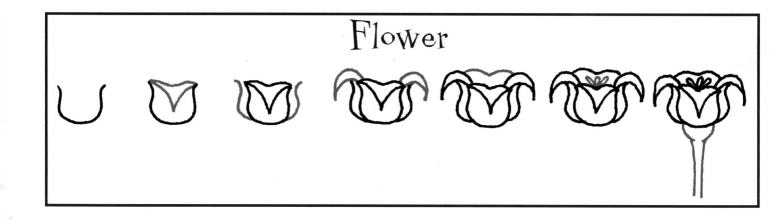

Bzzz . . . pollen break!

watercolor

Grasshopper

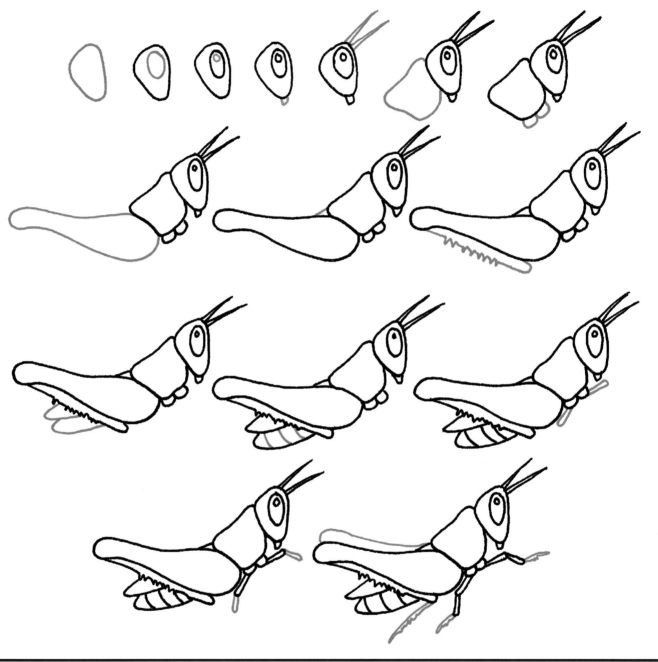

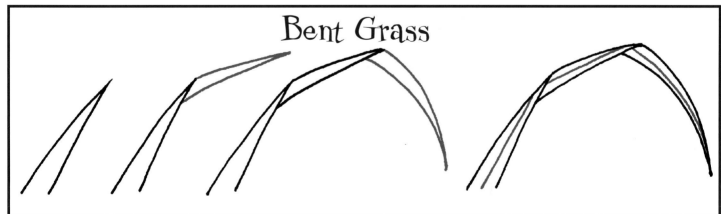

Bent Grass

Your grasshopper sure looks good
on that blade of grass.

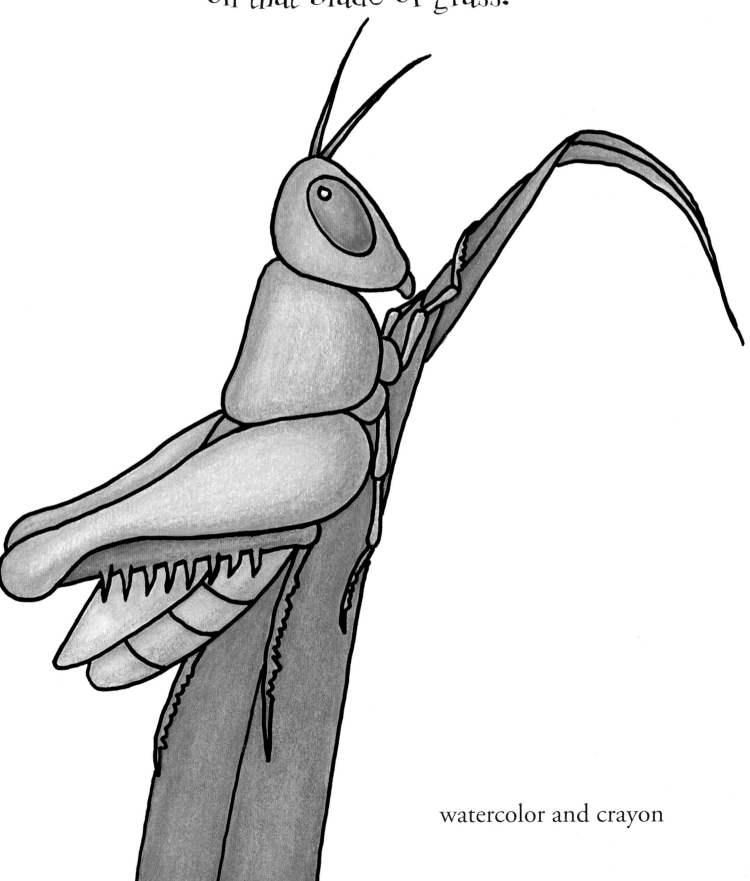

watercolor and crayon

Dragonfly

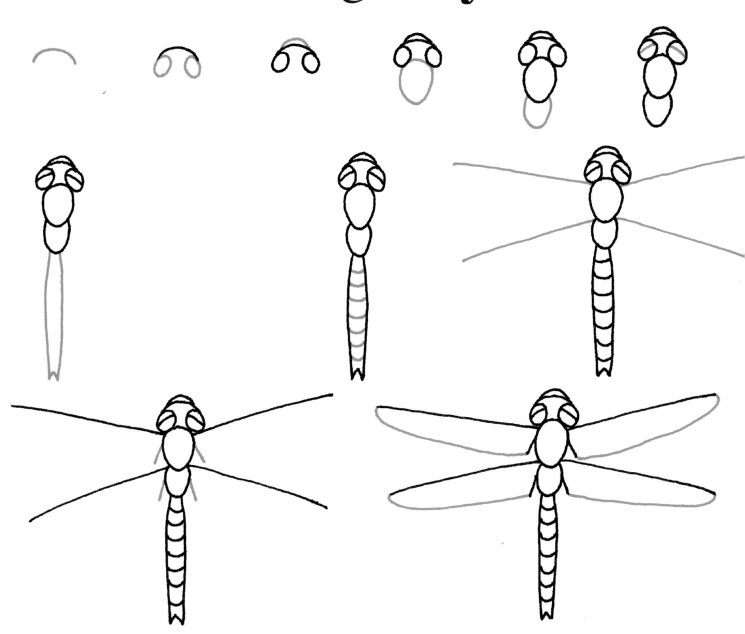

Realistic Wings

Try overlapping the dragonfly wings.

watercolor and colored pencil

Praying Mantis

Branch

Hey, look! The praying mantis grew more legs!

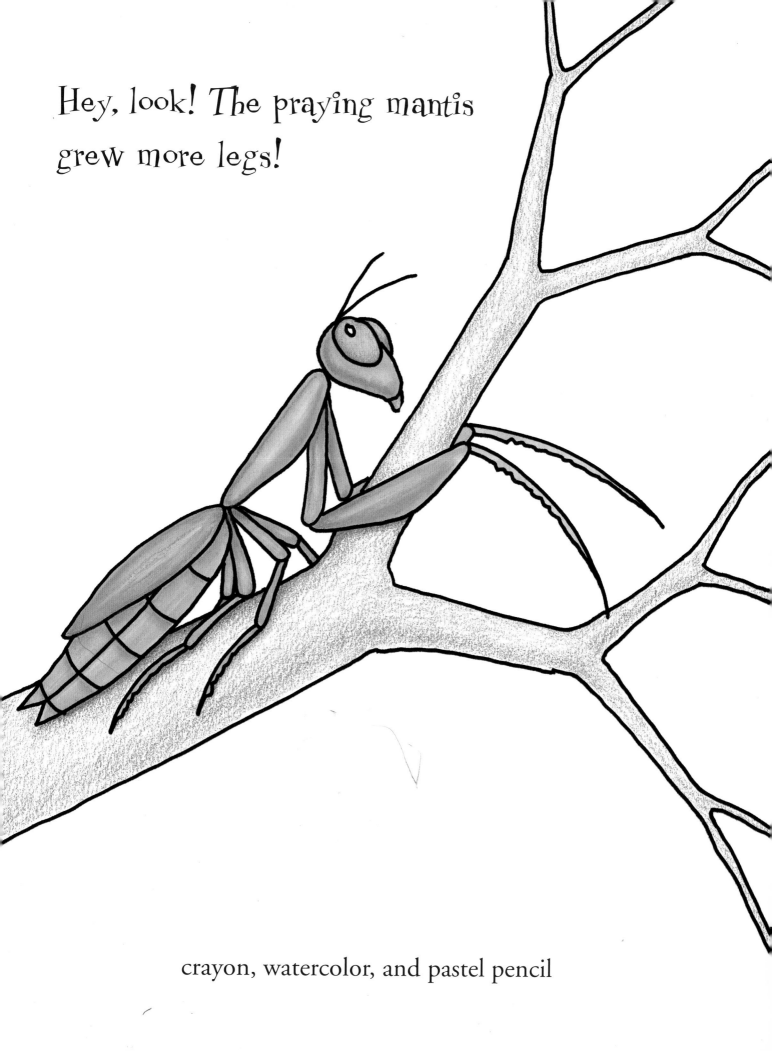

crayon, watercolor, and pastel pencil

Time to use your imagination.

Now that you've mastered drawing some realistic bugs, why not try and create your own imaginary bugs? Use what you've learned as a starting point. Then name your bugs and write stories about them.

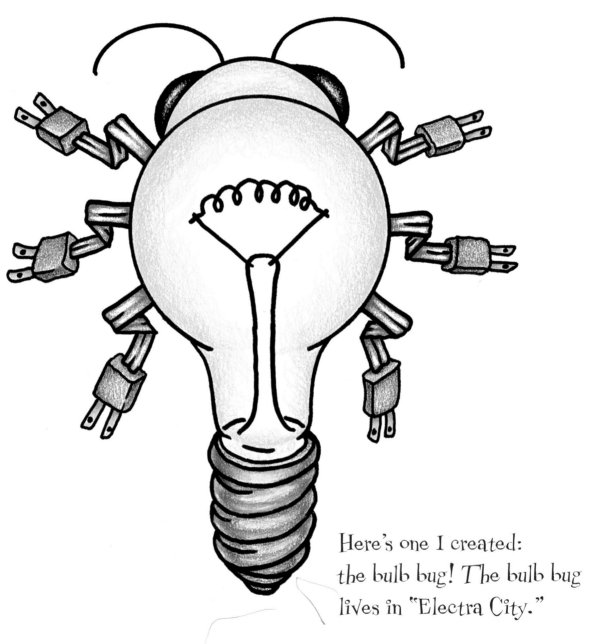

Here's one I created: the bulb bug! The bulb bug lives in "Electra City."

Have fun, and keep on drawing!